THE NEED TO KNOW LIBRARY™

EVERYTHING YOU NEED TO KNOW ABOUT
THE RISKS OF UNPROTECTED SEX

CAROLYN DECARLO

Rosen
YA™

New York

Published in 2019 by The Rosen Publishing Group, Inc.
29 East 21st Street, New York, NY 10010

Library of Congress Cataloging-in-Publication Data

Names: DeCarlo, Carolyn, author.
Title: Everything you need to know about the risks of unprotected sex / Carolyn DeCarlo.
Description: New York : Rosen Publishing, 2019 | Series: The need to know library | Audience: Grades 7–12. | Includes bibliographical references and index.
Identifiers: LCCN 2018011696| ISBN 9781508183617 (library bound) | ISBN 9781508183600 (pbk.)
Subjects: LCSH: Unsafe sex—Juvenile literature. | Sex instruction for children—Juvenile literature.
Classification: LCC HQ76 .D425 2019 | DDC 306.77—dc23
LC record available at https://lccn.loc.gov/2018011696

Manufactured in the United States of America

CONTENTS

INTRODUCTION

You wake up in an unfamiliar place. Or maybe your surroundings are familiar, but your body feels different. Perhaps you're in your own bed at home and your body feels fine, but your head is sore. You know something happened the night before but you can't remember what it was. Then you start to remember. You and your partner got carried away. It may have been a mutual decision or you may have felt forced. You may not quite remember how it happened. Maybe you were confidently going along with it, caught up in the moment, or under the influence of drugs or alcohol. However it happened, you're starting to feel a bit panicky. Your heart feels like it skips a beat or two as it sinks in: you had unprotected sex. Now what?

You are probably feeling an array of emotions, no matter how it happened. Your partner may still be lying next to you, but you might not feel comfortable asking him or her for help. Or he or she may be gone, and you are reflecting on this alone. Or maybe you talk about this together and agree that you both need to do something about this mistake. But what are the possible consequences? And what can you do?

If you have had unprotected sex, you may be at risk for a sexually transmitted infection (STI, sometimes known as a sexually transmitted disease, or STD), human immunodeficiency virus (HIV), and—depending on the situation—pregnancy. It is important for you to get

If you just had unprotected sex, you may be dealing with a lot of questions related to yourself and your partner. Do not panic! There are steps you can take.

tested for STIs before having any more sexual relations. It is a good idea to get tested immediately after having unprotected sex. However, some diseases, such as HIV, take a while to show up in a blood test, so you should also go back for another round of tests at a later date.

If pregnancy is a concern for you or your partner, you may want to consider obtaining emergency contraception such as Plan B (levonorgestrel), otherwise known as the "morning-after pill." This is birth control that can prevent pregnancy after unprotected sex, and it is more effective the sooner you take it. You can get Plan B over the counter without a prescription, regardless of your age or gender, and you may be able to get it for free from Planned Parenthood or a health care provider. Although pharmacists are legally allowed to refuse to give you Plan B, they are supposed to refer you to another pharmacy that can provide it.

Realizing you've had unprotected sex is certainly very scary. No matter what path you take, it is important for you to know that you are not alone. Learning more about your options can help you face the next steps.

CHAPTER ONE

WHAT IS UNPROTECTED SEX?

Unprotected sex means having sex (whether it be vaginal, anal, or oral) without using a condom. When two people decide to have sex, they should be prepared, protect themselves, and consider any possible consequences. Choosing to have unprotected sex of any kind puts your body at risk of contracting HIV and other STIs. Protecting yourself against STIs, HIV, and unplanned pregnancy is incredibly important, empowering, and not too hard as long as you have all the right information.

HOW DO STIS SPREAD?

Most STIs are spread through intimate bodily contact or exchange of fluids. There is a risk of STI in any sexual encounter in which a body that is carrying an STI comes into direct physical contact with another body.

Sex can be defined in a variety of different ways. Some people think of sex simply as a penis going

WHAT'S THE BIG DEAL ABOUT STIS?

According to a 2017 report by the Centers for Disease Control and Prevention (CDC), 110 million people in the United States have an STI. Perhaps even more alarmingly, 85 percent of Americans living with genital herpes don't even know they have the virus. The CDC also estimates that 19 million people contract STIs each year, and almost half of those people are between fifteen and twenty-four years old. At least 50 percent of sexually active adults will have a human papilloma virus (HPV) infection at some point

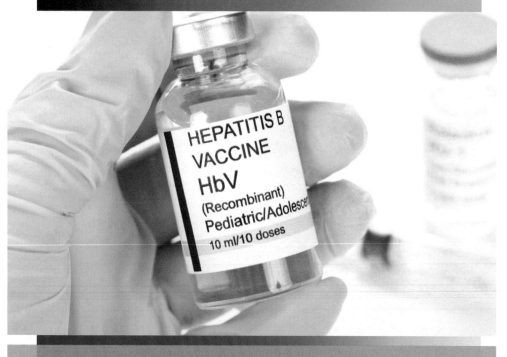

Hepatitis B cannot be cured, but it can be prevented with a vaccine. The vaccine is recommended by the CDC for all infants and children up to eighteen years old.

in their lives, but in 90 percent of those cases, the body's immune system will fight off the disease within two years.

When it comes to HIV, more than 1.2 million Americans are living with the disease, and one in eight of those aren't aware that they're infected. More than 12 million Americans (or, one in twenty people) have been infected by hepatitis B. There are nearly 100,000 new cases each year, while approximately 5,000 Americans die from the virus and its complications each year. As for bacterial infections like chlamydia and gonorrhea—which are both treatable with a round of antibiotics—less than half of new infections are not reported because there are no symptoms so the carriers don't even know they have them.

into a vagina, but this is not the only way humans have sex. Aside from vaginal sex (penis-in-vagina intercourse), some different forms of sex include oral sex (mouth-to-genital contact), anal sex (penis-in-anus intercourse), fingering or "hand jobs" (hand-to-genital contact), or "dry humping" or genital rubbing (contact between the genitals without penetration).

Not all these types of sex can lead to pregnancy or the spread of HIV, but all of them do carry some risk for picking up an STI. Some STIs can even be spread via sex toys, so it is important to properly clean and disinfect any sex toys that have been used by another person. Another option is to put a condom on a sex toy or, ideally, not share sex toys at all.

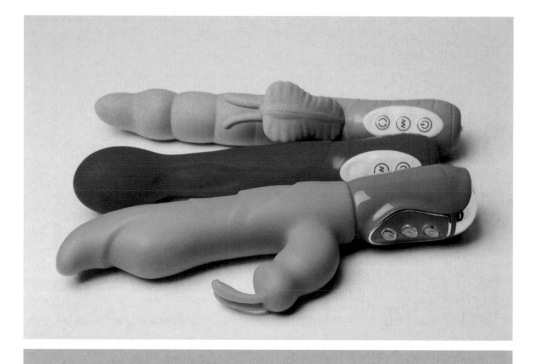

Sex toys can be used when alone or with partners. Either way, it is important to clean them between uses to prevent bacterial growth.

WHY DO PEOPLE HAVE UNPROTECTED SEX?

People can end up having unprotected sex for a number of reasons. Sometimes alcohol, drugs, and peer pressure can lead people to make decisions that they later regret. Sometimes young people do not understand how to protect themselves because they have not received adequate sex education in school. Additionally, the stigma around sex can make it hard for people of all ages to communicate about what they want and what they're comfortable with.

If you are mature enough to be having sex, you should be mature enough to talk about it. This means communicating about what you like and don't like and how you're going to protect each other from STIs and pregnancy. It should not be the responsibility of one partner alone—it should be something you discuss and agree on together. This applies whether you are in a long-term relationship or you're about to have sex with someone you just met that night.

This stigma around sex particularly impacts girls and women, who are often seen as sluts for being sexually active or for wanting to have sex. Meanwhile, boys can have sex with multiple partners without judgment. This sexual double standard is unfair, and it means that some girls do not feel comfortable talking about protection or carrying condoms. But there is no shame in carrying condoms and being prepared. In fact, it's the only way to stay safe.

It is also perfectly OK to not want to have sex. In a sex-obsessed culture, many teens feel like they have to be sexually active just because their friends are, but you should never have sex just because you feel that you should. It is important to listen to your body and know your own boundaries when it comes to sex. This means knowing what you want to do, no matter what someone else suggests or tells you to do.

It is also very important to understand consent and to respect your partner's boundaries. Most people have heard the slogan "no means no," but truly understanding consent means more than just listening out for the word no. If a person doesn't say no but seems uncertain or is

Preventing sexual violence begins with truly understanding what consent means. This starts with opening up true channels of communication between sexual partners.

too drunk or tired to notice what's happening—that is not consent. Sex should feel good to both people.

Consent applies to protection as well. Both partners should agree on what form or forms of protection to use. You should never pressure somebody into having sex without a condom for any reason. If someone tries to pressure you into having sex without a condom, it's a sign that that person doesn't respect you and isn't worthy of your trust.

METHODS OF PROTECTION

One way to protect yourself from STIs and pregnancy is not to have sex. If you don't want to have sex, then abstinence is a great choice for you. It is 100 percent effective in protecting you from STIs and pregnancy—except in the case of rape or sexual assault. However, if you do want to have sex, you will need to learn how to protect yourself and your partner from STIs, HIV, and unplanned pregnancy. Remember that if you are abstaining from sexual intercourse but engaging in other kinds of sexual activity (for example oral sex or hand jobs), you are still at risk for some STIs.

If you are using condoms, it is important to choose the right fit for you and your partner.

If you are having sexual intercourse (sex involving a penis penetrating a vagina, anus, or mouth), the only way to protect yourself from HIV and many other STIs is to use a condom. This could be an external/"male" condom or an internal/"female" condom. But even condoms aren't 100 percent foolproof—condoms can break, and some STIs are transmitted by skin-to-skin contact, not through semen or other bodily fluids. Some condoms, such as lambskin condoms, protect against pregnancy but do not protect against STIs and HIV.

In certain cases, people who are particularly at risk for getting HIV may take a course of drugs called pre-exposure prophylaxis (PrEP), which can lower a person's chance of HIV infection.

To protect against pregnancy, many people use condoms in addition to other birth control methods such as the Pill, IUD, birth control patch, or birth control shot.

SAFER SEX IS NOT SAFE SEX

Using condoms every time you have sex drastically reduces your chances of getting an STI or getting pregnant, but it does not completely eliminate the risks. For this reason, if you are sexually active, you should get tested for STIs on a regular basis. Many STIs don't have symptoms, so you could be carrying an infection without even knowing it. Getting tested can provide peace of mind, give you the knowledge you need to help yourself and your future partners, and help to curb the spread of STIs.

MYTHS AND FACTS

MYTH: Removing my pubic hair will clear away any pubic lice.

FACT: Although it's true that you don't need to visit a clinic or see a doctor, you will need to purchase an insecticide cream, lotion, or shampoo from the pharmacy to get rid of pubic lice. You do not need a prescription and you can treat yourself at home. Read the application instructions closely or ask a pharmacist or doctor if you are not sure what to do.

MYTH: HIV can be spread through mosquito bites.

FACT: HIV is only found in humans. It cannot be passed through contact with animals or insect bites (including from mosquitoes). It is not possible to get HIV from toilet seats, swimming pools, towels, sheets, or clothing. It is just as safe to share things that people with HIV have touched or kitchen utensils they've used as it is to kiss, shake hands with, or hug them. The virus cannot pass through unbroken skin and it is not spread via saliva, tears, sweat, urine, or feces.

MYTH: Lambskin condoms are a great alternative for anyone who may be allergic to latex condoms.

FACT: While it is true that lambskin condoms do not contain latex and can be used by the latex sensitive, these condoms are effective only for protection against pregnancy. They do not protect against STIs. There are several other kinds of condoms available that are safe for those with latex allergies to use—made with polyisoprene or polyurethane—that offer protection against pregnancy as well as STIs.

CHAPTER TWO

SYMPTOMS AND SIGNS

STIs are picked up and passed on primarily during sex. STIs are caused by bacteria, viruses, or parasites. The best thing you can do to avoid an STI is to use protection (in the form of a condom) every single time you have sex. However, condoms aren't guaranteed to protect you from STIs. If you do have unprotected sex, if a condom breaks, or if you are a victim of rape or sexual assault, you will need to know how to recognize the signs of STIs.

BACTERIAL INFECTIONS

Bacterial STIs include gonorrhea, chlamydia, syphilis, chancroid, lymphogranuloma venerium (LGV), mycoplasma genitalium, nongonococcal urethritis (NGU), pelvic inflammatory disease (PID), and vaginitis. The best-known STIs caused by bacteria are gonorrhea, chlamydia, and syphilis.

GONORRHEA

Gonorrhea is caused by bacteria that live in warm, damp parts of the body, including the throat, penis, vagina, and rectum. If left unchecked, the bacteria can cause infertility. Gonorrhea may be spread by contact with the vagina, penis, mouth, or anus or with semen and vaginal fluids. It can take as long as thirty days for symptoms to appear, and some people never have symptoms. According to the New York State Department of Health, 80 percent of women who have gonorrhea do not have symptoms, but they can still spread the dis-

There are many ways of passing on an STI besides through sexual intercourse. Get tested regardless of your partnership status or history.

ease. In the penis, gonorrhea causes yellow, white, or green discharge, swelling of the foreskin, and a burning feeling while urinating. Symptoms in the vagina include changes in discharge, burning urination, and bleeding between periods. Gonorrhea in the throat and rectum is generally symptom free. Gonorrhea is commonly spread through vaginal, oral, and anal sex. It can also be spread through unsterilized sex toys, or by skin-to-skin contact of the infected area.

CHLAMYDIA

Chlamydia often presents without any initial symptoms, but it can become serious when left untreated. It is produced by bacteria found in infected semen and vaginal fluids. In general, women and other female-bodied people with chlamydia do not have symptoms, and only 50 percent of men or male-bodied people do, according to the CDC. When symptoms do appear, they include whitish, cloudy, or watery discharge from the penis, a change in vaginal discharge, and pain when urinating. Chlamydia can cause pain in the stomach or lower back during sex, between periods, or after sex. Chlamydia in the throat and rectum are generally symptom-free. Chlamydia is spread during vaginal, oral, and anal sex, by skin-to-skin contact of the affected area, and by sharing sex toys. Chlamydia can also be transferred to the eyes, where it can cause conjunctivitis.

SYPHILIS

Syphilis is a bacterial infection that spreads easily through oral, anal, and vaginal sex. It can cause serious damage to the heart, brain, and nervous system if

DO I HAVE PARASITES?

Parasites cause pubic lice and scabies, both of which may be transmitted without sexual contact. Pubic lice or "crabs" are small crab-shaped insects that can grow to the size of a pinhead and feed on blood. They are usually irritating, particularly in the nighttime. They live on body hair, including pubic hair, underarm hair, leg hair, chest hair, and even eyebrows or facial hair, but not on the scalp.

Usually the following symptoms show up several weeks after getting pubic lice: itching (potentially

(continued on the next page)

Pubic lice grow to the size of a pinhead and can be seen by the naked eye. They are insects but are often called crabs because of the way they look under a microscope.

(continued from the previous page)

intense) in the affected areas, irritated skin, bites on the skin and the presence of blood caused by lice bites, blue specks on the skin, and black powder from lice droppings in underclothes. The lice themselves, or their eggs, may also be seen. Pubic lice are most commonly passed through body contact, particularly during sex. However, they can also be passed during hugging or kissing, on clothing, sheets, towels, or even toilet seats.

left untreated. It has three stages, all with distinct symptoms. The first (primary) stage occurs ten days to three months after infection in the form of a painless sore at the site of infection—usually on the genitals, mouth, or rectum. It may be accompanied by swelling. This heals after around two to six weeks, if untreated, and is followed quickly by the second (secondary) stage, which involves a body rash appearing particularly on the hands and soles of the feet. This stage may also include fever, headache, hair loss, weight loss, and growths similar to genital warts. After this stage, the infection becomes dormant; then, years later, the third (tertiary) phase appears, causing damage to the infected person's heart, brain, and nervous system. Syphilis is passed through unprotected oral, vaginal, and anal sex and through contact with the primary sores or secondary rash. It can also be passed through the sharing of sex toys and from a parent to an infant during childbirth. Untreated, syphilis can be spread for up to two years after the latent period has begun.

VIRAL INFECTIONS

Common viral STIs include herpes, HPV, hepatitis, and HIV. These viral STIs typically cause more alarm than bacterial STIs because they often stay with a person for life.

HERPES

Herpes is caused by the herpes simplex virus (HSV). There are two types—HSV1 and HSV2. In general,

HSV1 causes oral herpes, which may appear as blisters or cold sores on the mouth and lips. While common and often inactive, it is important to be open with anyone you plan to kiss.

HSV1 causes oral herpes (infection of the mouth) and sometimes genital herpes, and HSV2 causes genital herpes. HSV1 is spread by kissing, while HSV2 is usually spread during vaginal or anal sex. It can also pass from one person's genitals to another person's mouth, causing oral herpes. Many people are infected with herpes without knowing it. While usually inactive, the virus remains in the body for life. Every so often, the virus is reactivated causing an outbreak.

Both types of herpes can cause blisters. They appear as cold sores on the mouth, throat, thighs, and buttocks; as genital herpes; and as whitlows (a type of painful abscess) on the fingers and hands. They can also trigger flulike aches and swollen glands and cause itchy, tingly, or numb patches on the skin. The blisters contain a transparent, infectious liquid that will open up, scab back over, and ultimately heal within two to four weeks of any outbreak. Infection, which is more common during outbreak, is also passed by sharing sex toys and from an infected parent to the baby during childbirth.

HPV

Human papillomavirus (HPV) is not one virus but a strain of viruses. Each strain of HPV has its own number or type, and some types are more dangerous than others. According to the CDC, at least forty of the one hundred types of HPV can be transmitted during sexual contact.

Low-risk strains of HPV, such as types 6 and 11, cause genital warts. Warts are small fleshlike growths, bumps, or skin changes found anywhere on the genitals, anus, or upper thighs. They are usually not painful or a serious threat to one's health. Many people may not know the warts are there if they are inside the anus, vagina, or on the cervix. There may be just one or a cluster (which may appear similar to a cauliflower). Warts may develop weeks, months, or even years after infection and can be episodic or recurring. Though painless, they may itch, become inflamed, or bleed. If left untreated, they may go away—but there is a chance they could remain unchanged or even grow larger.

High-risk strains of HPV, such as types 16 and 18, can lead to cervical cancer. HPV is transmitted during sex when one person's skin touches another person's warts (either outside or inside of the body). It can be spread through penetrative sex, genital contact, sharing sex toys, and, occasionally, during oral sex. The virus may be passed while no warts are present.

Vaccines are available for the prevention of some of the more serious strains of HPV. These vaccines—Cervarix, Gardasil, and Gardasil 9—are available for children of all genders as young as nine years old and for adults up to age twenty-six.

HEPATITIS

Hepatitis is an inflammation of the liver. There are five viruses known to cause hepatitis, but the three main types are hepatitis A, hepatitis B, and hepatitis C. Types B and C are increasingly common among people living with HIV. Hepatitis infection can be acute or chronic. Acute means it lasts less than six months and may or may not come with symptoms. Sometimes acute hepatitis progresses into chronic (long-term) hepatitis and can cause lasting damage to the liver, including liver failure or cancer.

Hepatitis A is most often transmitted by way of contaminated food or water, but it can also be transmitted during sexual activities. Mild symptoms, including diarrhea, nausea, exhaustion, itchy skin, abdominal pain, and jaundice, may occur up to six weeks after infection and can last several weeks. Hepatitis A may be transmitted through fecal matter, through food prepared by an infected person, or through contaminated water. The virus must get into the mouth to cause infection, which may happen during sex if traces of feces appear on the fingers or anus.

Many people with hepatitis B have no symptoms. Others may have symptoms lasting several weeks including mild loss of appetite, fever, extreme tiredness, nausea or vomiting, stomach pain, and jaundice. Up to one in twenty infected people become carriers, meaning they have chronic hepatitis and a continued risk of infecting others or developing liver disease. Around one in one hundred people get a more serious illness, which can be fatal when not treated immediately. Hepatitis B is transmitted through bodily fluids including blood, semen, pre-ejaculate, and vaginal secretions. It can also be acquired through unprotected oral, vaginal, or anal sex, shared sex toys, shared needles and syringes that contain infected blood, and from parent to baby during childbirth. If you know someone with an infection or if you are infected yourself, do not share tweezers, clippers, razors, or toothbrushes, as trace amounts of blood may pass on the virus. This powerful virus can survive for a week independent of the body in things like dried blood.

Hepatitis C is caused by a blood-borne virus that targets the liver and spreads easily through sex and the sharing of drug-injecting instruments (e.g. needles and syringes). Pregnant people can

Some STIs such as hepatitis and HIV can be passed from parent to child during pregnancy, childbirth, or breastfeeding.

give the virus to their babies before or during childbirth. Without treatment, hepatitis C can cause fatal liver disease. According to the CDC, around 15 to 30 percent of people with hepatitis C naturally get rid of the virus during the acute phase, the first six months of infection. Those who do not get rid of the virus in the first six months enter the chronic (long-term) phase. Symptoms of hepatitis C include mild flulike symptoms, nausea, extreme tiredness, itchy skin, stomach pain, jaundice, mental confusion (called brain fog), and depression. Unfortunately, most people do not realize when they're first infected, and it may take years before they start to feel sick.

HIV

The human immunodeficiency virus (HIV) was first identified in the 1980s, though it was prevalent in up to five continents before that. "Immunodeficiency" refers to the fact that the virus reduces a person's immune system, which is the part of the body that fights diseases. HIV is the virus itself; acquired immune deficiency syndrome (AIDS) is the name for a collection of illnesses caused by the virus.

When first infected, many people notice no symptoms. However, in the first six weeks, most people experience a short illness (called seroconversion illness) that lasts approximately two weeks, during which the body reacts to the virus. This involves a body rash, sore throat, and fever. Seroconversion is the point at which the body produces antibodies to HIV. While most infected people get the illness, some experience cases so mild they mistake it for the flu. After this, many years may pass before an infected person feels any other effects.

In a person with HIV, his or her bodily fluids (including blood, semen, vaginal, and anal secretions) are highly infectious—particularly during the weeks and months after initial infection. Also, as HIV weakens the immune system and the T-cell (CD4) count drops, people may experience signs associated with other illnesses, such as weight loss, night sweats, oral thrush, increase in cold sore outbreaks, swollen glands, diarrhea, and tiredness.

HIV is transmitted when infected fluid from blood, semen, vaginal fluid, anal mucus, or breast milk passes from one body to another. This may occur when injecting drugs, during pregnancy, or during vaginal or anal sex. If left untreated, the virus can cause a lot of damage through several life-threatening illnesses known as AIDS-defining illnesses, including cancer, tuberculosis (TB), and pneumonia. (The term "syndrome" means a collection of illnesses.) This is because HIV is quietly destroying the cells the immune systems need to protect the body from infection.

CHAPTER THREE

HOW DO I STAY SAFE?

There are many different ways to have sex, and not all STIs are spread the same way. There is not one method of protection that works for every situation, but there are some methods that are much more effective than others.

BIRTH CONTROL

When it comes to birth control, condoms prevent sperm from reaching the vagina so sperm can't join with an egg and develop into pregnancy. If you used condoms flawlessly every time, they would be 98 percent effective at preventing pregnancy. But no human is perfect, so in reality, condoms are approximately 85 percent effective. This means about fifteen out of one hundred people who use condoms as their solitary method of birth control will get pregnant in any given year, according to Planned Parenthood.

There are many other birth control methods that can be very effective if used correctly. The birth control pill

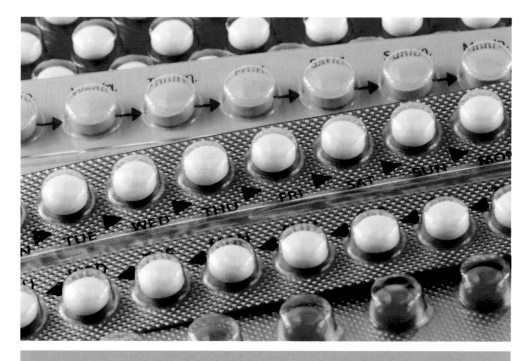

The birth control pill is an effective contraceptive when taken every day, but it involves a level of daily responsibility that other methods such as IUDs and the birth control patch do not.

is 91 percent effective at preventing pregnancy, the birth control implant and the IUD are both 99 percent effective, and the birth control shot is 94 percent effective, according to Planned Parenthood. There's also the birth control patch, sponge, vaginal ring, diaphragm, and other methods. Remember to use condoms in addition to one of these other birth control methods because condoms are the only method that protects you from STIs as well as pregnancy.

If you have unprotected sex or you use a condom but it tears and you are concerned about becoming pregnant, you may choose to take emergency contraception such as Plan B, also known as the morning-after pill. This type of birth control can prevent pregnancy after unprotected sex, and it is more effective the sooner you take it. Plan B is available over the counter without a prescription, and you may be able to get it for free from Planned Parenthood or another health care provider.

THE RIGHT WAY TO PUT ON A CONDOM

Condoms protect against STIs by covering the penis, inhibiting contact with semen and vaginal fluids, and limiting skin-to-skin contact that can increase the spread of STIs. Using condoms every time for oral, anal, and vaginal sexual intercourse is the best way to reduce the chances of spreading STIs. Condoms safeguard you and your partners from STIs by inhibiting contact with all bodily fluids that might be carrying infection. And because condoms create a barrier, they help protect against certain STIs, such as herpes and genital warts, which are spread via skin-to-skin contact.

If you have a penis or if you intend to have sex with someone who has a penis, you should learn how to correctly put on a condom. First, check that the condom has not passed its expiration or "use by" date, printed on the wrapper. An unopened condom should last up to five years when it is properly stored. Do not rip the condom when removing it from its wrapper. Make sure the condom is facing the right way up by placing it over a fingertip. The rim should be on the outside so that it looks like a little hat. If it does not roll down easily, turn it over before putting it on the penis.

If the condom is inside out once it's already on, remove it and use a new one, as there could be some semen on it. The penis must be fully erect before you put on the condom, otherwise it may not stay in place. Do not unroll or stretch the condom before it is in position. If the condom has a teat at the tip, be sure to squeeze any remaining air out of it. No air or lubricant should be trapped under the condom. Using an even and steady motion, unroll the condom until it has reached the base of the penis.

There are a few other things you should know about condoms:

- After half an hour of use, replace the condom with a new one to avoid tearing.
- Make sure that the condom hasn't come off inside the vagina or anus. After ejaculation, hold the base of the penis (and the condom) firmly before pulling out.
- Don't reuse condoms. Use a new condom if switching from one kind of sex to another (for example, vaginal to anal) or if having sex with a different person.
- Don't use more than one condom at the same time or they are likely to tear.
- Use water-based or silicone-based lube with a condom. Never use an oil-based lube, which can make the condom split. Don't spit on the condom. Spit dries fast, leaving the condom prone to breaking.

WHEN SEX IS NOT A CHOICE

If you have been a victim of rape or sexual assault, seek a service provider right away. If you consented to sex with a condom but the person you're having sex with took off the condom, that is also a form of sexual assault, and it's never OK. Coping with the trauma of rape or sexual assault is hard enough without the added worry that you may have been infected or become pregnant. It can be overwhelming to know where to turn for help.

A good first step is calling the National Sexual Assault Hotline at 1-800-656-HOPE (4673). This twenty-four-hour confidential service has trained specialists who can answer your questions about receiving medical attention, reporting the offense, and choosing whether a sexual assault forensic exam, sometimes known as a rape kit, is right for you. You can also get confidential twenty-four-hour help online at online.rainn.org.

INTERNAL CONDOMS OR FEMIDOMS

While external condoms are the most commonly used form of prevention against STIs, the internal female condom, or "femidom," is an equally effective method for blocking pregnancy and the transmission of STIs like HIV. Instead of going on the penis, it is inserted into the vagina as an alternative to the external condom. Usually, it is produced from a synthetic material like nitrile and has a flexible ring at each end: one inside, the other near the vaginal opening.

The internal condom, also known as the femidom, allows people with vaginas to have more control over their sexual health and safety.

To insert it, squeeze the inner ring between your thumb and finger to make it long and narrow—this makes it easier to insert. With the inner ring between your fingers, insert the femidom as deep as it will go. Insert your middle finger into the femidom and push the inner ring as far into your vagina as you can, so that it is resting above the pubic bone. The outer ring should remain outside the opening of the vagina. During sex, guide the shaft of the penis or sex toy in through the outer ring, making sure it hasn't passed outside the opening of the condom and entered on the wrong side of the ring. After use, twist the outer ring of the condom before you remove it. This makes it harder for semen or any other fluid to spill out of it.

Internal condoms may be inserted several hours before sex. They may be a good option for partners of people who find that external condoms reduce sensation. Some people use internal condoms for anal sex, although this is not their designated purpose. There are no studies on their reliability for anal use.

DENTAL DAMS, PLASTIC WRAP, AND CUT-OPEN CONDOMS

For types of sex that do not involve penetration with a penis, such as cunnilingus (oral contact with female genitals) or rimming (oral contact with the anus), there are other barrier methods that can protect from STIs. These include dental dams, plastic wrap, and cut-open condoms. While some of these methods are not FDA approved, they have been endorsed by Planned Parenthood and the CDC.

A dental dam is a small plastic sheet that can be used to cover the mouth, vagina, or anus to reduce the risk of STIs and HIV during oral sex. While most dental dams were not created for STI prevention, the Sheer Glyde Dam was created specifically for this purpose and is FDA approved for oral sex on female genitals. External condoms can also be cut open along the side and placed over the vulva to provide a barrier during oral sex. Some people even use plastic wrap that they buy at the grocery store to place over the vulva, anus, or mouth during non-penetrative oral sex for protection against STIs.

AIDS.gov recommends using nonmicrowaveable plastic wrap since microwave-safe plastic wrap has tiny holes in it, which might let bacteria and viruses through.

PREP AND PEP: REDUCING THE RISK OF HIV

HIV treatment can act as a form of protection as it stops HIV from being transmitted. Pre-exposure prophylaxis (PrEP) is a course of HIV drugs taken by people who do not have HIV in order to lower their chance of infection. When used properly, PrEP significantly reduces a person's chances of becoming HIV positive. Pre-exposure

It is important to communicate with your partner about all kinds of sexual protection. Many STIs can be transmitted during oral sex, which is why the Sheer Glyde Dam was invented.

prophylaxis (PrEP) are antiretroviral drugs. They are taken daily, and are only prescribed to people deemed to be at a very high risk for HIV infection. To prevent sexual transmission of HIV, PrEP may be suggested for someone engaging in an ongoing sexual relationship with an HIV-positive partner; anyone who is sexually active with multiple partners, even if they have tested negative for HIV; and men and women who have chosen not to use condoms with partners whose HIV status is unknown and qualify as being at an increased risk for HIV infection (for example, if they inject drugs). While PrEP can provide a high level of protection against HIV, it is most effective when used with condoms.

Post-exposure prophylaxis (PEP) is a month-long course of HIV medication that can be taken by people who do NOT have HIV after an event causing potential exposure, such as unprotected sex, to reduce their chances of getting HIV. It must begin within seventy-two hours of potential exposure. When taken in time, PEP can stop HIV infection from spreading after exposure with someone who is infectious. Unfortunately, it does not work every time. PEP is not 100 percent effective, and it should never be viewed as an appropriate substitute for condoms.

CHAPTER FOUR

I HAD UNPROTECTED SEX. NOW WHAT?

There are many reasons why people might engage in unprotected sex. Maybe you thought you were immune to STIs, or you didn't realize STIs could be transmitted via oral sex. Maybe a condom broke, or maybe your partner pressured you to have sex without one. You may have been intoxicated, tired, or lazy. In any case, unless you know for sure that your partner has recently tested negative for all STIs, you should get tested. Even if your partner says he or she has been tested, he or she may be lying or may just not know. Many STIs have no signs or symptoms.

Many people assume that their annual medical check-up covers STI tests. Some health care providers may run standard tests, but there is no way to be sure without asking. If you are worried you have been exposed to an STI, talk to your health care provider about getting tested for these common STIs: chlamydia, gonorrhea, HIV, herpes, HPV, syphilis, and trichomoniasis (commonly known as trich). You can arrange for testing with your health care provider or find a testing clinic near you. You can visit the American Sexual Health

Association website and enter your zip code to find a clinic near you: www.ASHAAexualHealth.org/stdsstis /get-tested.

HOW DO STI TESTS WORK?

The test for chlamydia involves a swab of the genital area or urine sample. If you have had oral or anal sex, let your healthcare provider know so that she can test these sites as well. It may seem embarrassing, but remember this is part of her job and she hears these things every day. The test for gonorrhea also involves

It is common to feel embarrassed talking to your doctor about your sexual health. Just remember, you're not the only person on the planet having sex. Even your doctor has to get tested!

a swab of the genital area or a urine sample. As with chlamydia, tell your health care provider if you have had oral or anal sex.

If you are getting a test for genital herpes but you have no symptoms, blood will be drawn from the arm or a finger. It is also important to ask for a type-specific IgG test and not an IgM test. If you are showing symptoms of genital herpes, the test can be done with a swab of the affected area. However, if that comes back negative (meaning no herpes virus is found), then it is important to follow up with a blood test. This must be done as soon as possible because a viral culture test is not as accurate after forty-eight hours. A negative culture does not mean that you do not have genital herpes.

The test for syphilis involves a blood test or a sample taken from a sore, while the test for trich involves a swab of the infected area, a physical examination, or a sample of the discharge. Trich is harder to detect in men than in women. The CDC recommends that all pregnant people be tested for syphilis.

It's a good idea to get tested for HPV, which can manifest as either genital warts or cervical cancer. If you have genital warts, the doctor can assess this by looking at the infected area. Warts can form in people of all genders. If you think you may have cervical cancer, you should get a Pap test. If the test result is abnormal, you may need to have an HPV DNA test and a biopsy. Pap tests detect cervical cell changes, not HPV itself—though an abnormal test is often caused by HPV

If you've been exposed to an STI, particularly HIV, finding a supportive network may provide all the encouragement you need to get tested and stay positive.

infection. There is no test available for male-bodied people for these types of HPV.

HIV TEST METHODS

If you think you have been exposed to HIV and may be in the first stages of HIV infection, get tested. HIV tests involve a swab of the inside of the mouth or a blood test. Confidential and anonymous testing options are available in many clinics. There are also kits that you can buy to

FOUR SHORT WORDS THAT ARE SO HARD TO SAY

If you have an STI, it's important to tell all your sexual partners, even if you use protection every time. But saying the words "I have an STI" can be hard to do. Perhaps you're afraid of rejection or perhaps it's just too embarrassing. Some partners may feel that it's not necessary to disclose something like oral herpes or genital warts because they are so common. Others may feel that, if they are acting responsibly and using protection, it is their business and their partner doesn't need to know. But open communication is essential when it comes to safe, consensual sex. Even if you're just planning a one-time sexual encounter, you still have the responsibility to share this information.

It can help to practice how you're going to disclose your STI. If you're worried it will be a mood killer, you may want to say it ahead of time. Also remember that it's always OK to ask a sexual partner if he or she has an STI. Don't worry about offending the person. Your safety is more important.

test yourself at home. Some HIV tests can detect acute and recent infections, but others cannot. This is because most HIV tests detect antibodies (the proteins produced by your body in response to HIV) and not the HIV itself. It may take several weeks or even longer for these antibodies to generate. It's important to inform the technician at your testing site if you think infection may have happened recently. Tests that can detect acute infection will check for HIV RNA or p24 antigen. While most doctors and clinics providing a full range of health care services are able to do this test, some with only basic testing services may not be able to provide it. You can ask before your appointment to find out ahead of time whether or not they will be able to test you for acute HIV infection.

ONGOING TREATMENT

After you get tested, it's important to follow up about the results of your test and find out what treatment you need. There are a number of free and low-cost health clinics. The website Your STD Help has a clinic locator tool where you can enter your address to find your closest clinic: www.YourSTDHelp.com/free_clinic_locator.html.

It's important to contact anyone you may have passed an infection along to—anyone you had sex with before getting tested—so that those people can get tested and treated, too. Many clinics will contact your former partners for you if this is something you don't feel comfortable doing yourself. They can do this anonymously, without giving your former partners your name.

TREATMENT FOR CHLAMYDIA, GONORRHEA, AND SYPHILIS

Bacterial infections such as chlamydia, gonorrhea, and syphilis are treated with antibiotics given in the form of

UNPLANNED PREGNANCY

If you think you may be pregnant, you can buy a pregnancy test at your local pharmacy or visit a health clinic to get tested. Finding yourself pregnant unintentionally can be a scary situation. You may decide you want to have the baby, or you may decide to give it up for adoption or have an abortion. You may have a strong sense of which option is right for you, or you may not be sure. In weighing your options, think about how each decision will impact your future, if you are ready to parent a child, and how much support you will receive from your friends, family, and partner.

(continued on the next page)

Confronting the possibility of an unplanned pregnancy can be difficult, but no matter the result of your pregnancy test, remember that you have options.

(continued from the previous page)

These are tough decisions to make by yourself, and it can be helpful to talk it through with a close friend or family member, your partner, or a counselor. Your local Planned Parenthood can also offer nonjudgmental support and help you talk through your options, as well as offering abortion, adoption, and prenatal care services. In the end, the decision is yours and yours alone, so don't let anyone pressure you to make a decision against your will.

tablets or injection. You should hold off on any sexual activities until the treatment has finished so the infection isn't passed to a partner. For a single dose of antibiotics, you'll be asked to wait one week before having sex. If left untreated, bacterial infections like chlamydia and gonorrhea may cause infertility. Syphilis can cause serious heart, brain, and nerve issues, which may develop years later.

TREATMENT FOR HERPES

The herpes virus stays inside your body for life, but antiviral tablets help avoid outbreaks, manage symptoms, and help heal any recurrences. If you have an unusually high number of outbreaks per year—more than six—you may have to take suppressive treatment on an ongoing basis. If you have fewer outbreaks, you will probably just need to take tablets during the outbreak itself. Pain-killing creams and salt water baths will help soothe any blisters that appear.

TREATMENT FOR HPV

Genital warts caused by the HPV virus must be treated by a doctor, and the sooner the better. Warts are removed with liquid nitrogen, laser treatment, surgery, or a special cream or acid that you can apply at a clinic or at home. Note that over-the-counter treatments for warts on the hands or feet are not suitable for HPV. It is important to wait until treatment has finished to resume having sex. It may take more than one treatment to remove the warts, and they may still reoccur.

The vaccine Gardasil protects against the two strains (types 6 and 11) of HPV that cause the majority of cases of genital warts, and two (types 16 and 18) that cause cervical cancer. Kids as young as nine years old can get the vaccine, but it is more commonly given at the age of eleven or twelve.

TREATMENT FOR HEPATITIS A, B, AND C

Most cases of hepatitis A and acute hepatitis B do not need treatment. The usual advice is rest and recovery. Once you've had hepatitis A or acute hepatitis B, you become immune and you can't catch it again, but you could still pass the infection through sex or things like preparation of food. It is important to let your partners know your status so they can get vaccinated.

Chronic hepatitis B is incurable, but it may be slowed down through treatment. A small number of carriers will get liver disease and cancer, and some may require a liver transplant.

The most common type of viral hepatitis is hepatitis C, which has no vaccine. The treatment for hepatitis C is to take direct-acting antivirals (DAAs) in the form of a tablet once or twice a day for twelve weeks. While 90 to 95 percent of people with hepatitis C can be cured, this does not make them immune to catching hepatitis C, or any other type of hepatitis, again.

HIV TREATMENT AND PREVENTION

If you are HIV positive, you should see a doctor and begin HIV treatment as soon as you can. There is a high risk for transmitting HIV during the first stage of HIV infection, even when you do not have symptoms. Because of this, you should take all possible steps to minimize the potential for transmitting the virus.

After the early stage of HIV infection, the disease moves into clinical latency, also known as chronic HIV infection. In this phase, HIV is active but reproducing at low levels. For people who aren't taking medicine to treat HIV, called antiretroviral therapy (ART), this period can last ten years or longer, but some may progress faster. People who are taking medicine to treat HIV and take it the right way, every

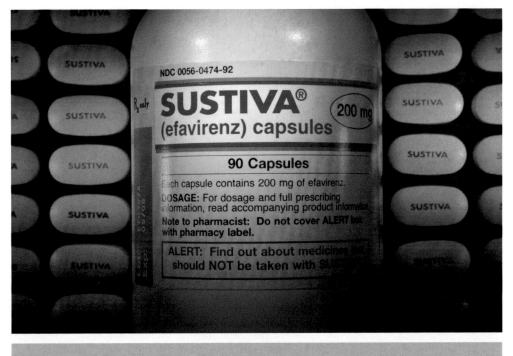

Efavirenz is an antiretroviral medication sold under the brand name Sustiva. It is commonly used to help treat HIV and prevent its progression into AIDS.

day, may be in this stage for several decades, as the treatment helps keep the virus in check. It is important to remember that HIV is still transmittable during this phase even without symptoms. However, people who are on ART and stay virally suppressed (or maintain a very low level of the virus in their blood) are much less able to spread HIV than those who are not. If you have HIV and you are not on ART, the virus will eventually weaken your body's immune system, and you will progress to AIDS, the late stage of HIV infection.

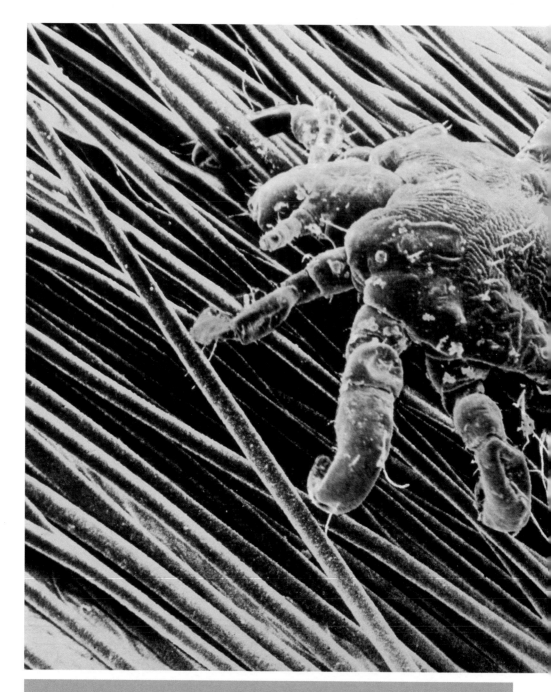

While both head lice and pubic lice can be treated with shampoos and other over-the-counter products, they are not the same pathogens and are not transmitted in the same ways.

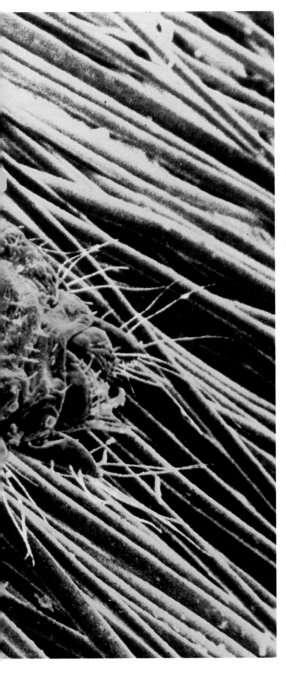

TREATMENT FOR PARASITES

If you have parasites such as pubic lice, you can treat them yourself without a visit to the doctor. Treatments such as insecticide cream, lotion, or shampoo such as Lyclear can be purchased over the counter from a pharmacy. Apply the treatment to the affected area, as well as any other hairy body parts. Read the instructions or ask a professional if you are unsure. If the lice have traveled to your eyelashes, you will need to see a doctor right away.

LIVING WITH AN STI

If you do have an STI that is not curable with treatment, it can be a

Contracting an incurable STI or HIV is not a death sentence, if treated correctly. Many people with STIs continue to live long and happy lives.

hard thing to handle emotionally. If you find yourself having trouble coming to terms with your diagnosis, tell a health care provider. She can evaluate your mental health and, if necessary, prescribe drugs, recommend therapy, or refer you to a psychiatrist. There are also a number of national and local support groups you can turn to. These groups are often based around a specific STI or group of STIs, such as the national HELP groups for those living with herpes or HPV. These groups may meet in person, online, or have a hotline you can call for answers to any questions you may have.

Remember that there is no shame in having an STI. Think about how many Americans are living with these infections and how many of them aren't even aware of it. When you get tested, your knowledge gives you power. With that power comes the responsibility to treat yourself and your future sexual partners with care and respect. By being responsible and honest, most people with STIs and HIV can continue to live full lives, including pleasurable sex lives.

GREAT QUESTIONS TO ASK A DOCTOR OR PHARMACIST

If I am in a committed monogamous relationship, do I still need to use condoms?

How do I tell my partner or potential future partners that I have an STI?

How old do I need to be to get on the Pill (or an IUD or other birth control method)? What about Plan B/the morning-after pill?

Can you contact my former partners to tell them I may have infected them?

Can I be tested for all STIs for my own peace of mind, or do I have to be able to prove I may be at risk?

If I test positive for HIV, will my name be entered onto a registry or recorded on a list somewhere?

If I have an STI or HIV, does that change my eligibility to do anything (such as holding a job, giving blood, or registering to vote)?

If I don't have health insurance, how can I get tested or treated for free?

How can I get free or low-cost birth control?

If I'm trying to get pregnant, how can I protect against STIs?

antibodies A substance produced by special cells that counteracts the effects of a disease germ or its poisons.

antiretroviral Acting, used, or effective against any single-stranded RNA virus (or retrovirus).

anus The lower opening of the digestive tract between a person's buttocks through which solid waste passes from the body.

assault A violent physical, sexual, or verbal attack.

asymptomatic Having or showing no symptoms of disease.

biopsy The removal of tissue, cells, or fluids from a living body in order to check for illness.

boundaries Limits that define acceptable behavior.

condom A layer commonly made of rubber designed to cover the penis to prevent conception and infection during sexual intercourse.

fetus A developing vertebrate from usually two months after conception to birth.

genitalia The organs of the reproductive system, particularly the external genital organs.

infection Any disease caused by germs entering the body.

lubrication Anything used to make something smooth and slippery in action or appearance.

mitigate To make less severe or painful; alleviate.

outbreak A sudden increase in numbers of a harmful organism, such as a disease.

parasite An organism that lives in, with, or on another organism.

protein Complex substances made up of many amino acids joined together that are essential for normal cell structure and function.

rectum The terminal part of the large intestine between the colon and the anus.

recurrence Occurring again after an interval, or over and over again.

teat A small projection or a nib, such as a nipple, through which milk is drawn from an udder or breast.

transmission The act or process of sending something from one person to another, such as with an infection.

uterus A muscular organ designed to contain and usually nourish a mammal's young during its development prior to birth.

vagina The passage within a mammal that leads from the uterus to the outside of the body.

virus The causative agent of an infectious disease.

vulva The external parts of the female genital organs.

American Liver Foundation
39 Broadway, Suite 2700
New York, NY 10006
(212) 668-1000
Website: https://www.liverfoundation.org
Facebook: @liverinfo
Twitter: @liverUSA
Instagram and YouTube: @americanliver
An organization that facilitates and promotes education,
    support, and research for the prevention, treatment
    and cure of liver disease, including hepatitis.

American Sexual Health Association (ASHA)
PO Box 13827
Research Triangle Park, NC 27709
(919) 361-8400
Website: http://www.ashasexualhealth.org
Twitter: @infoASHA
YouTube: @ashastd
ASHA encourages the sexual health of individuals,
    families, and communities by advocating for com-
    prehensive policies and practices and educating the
    public, professionals, and policy makers, in order to
    promote healthy sexual behaviors.

The Body: The Complete HIV/AIDS Resource
750 3rd Avenue, 6th Floor
New York, NY 10017

(212) 541-8500
Website: http://www.thebody.com
Facebook and Twitter: @thebodydotcom
An organization that works to lower barriers between patients and clinicians, demystify HIV/AIDS and its treatment, improve the quality of life for all people living with HIV/AIDS, and foster community through human connection.

Canadian AIDS Society (CAS)
190 O'Connor Street, Suite 100
Ottawa, ON K2P 2R3
Canada
(613) 230-3580
Website: http://www.cdnaids.ca
Facebook: @aidsida
Twitter and Instagram: @cdnaids
CAS represents community-based HIV/AIDS organizations across Canada, with the objective to strengthen the response to HIV/AIDS in Canada and enrich the lives of people and communities living with, and affected by, HIV/AIDS.

Sex and U
2781 Lancaster Road, Suite 200
Ottawa, ON K1B 1A7
Canada
(800) 561-2416
Website: https://www.sexandu.ca
Facebook: @sogc.org
Twitter: @SOGCorg

YouTube: @sexandu

This organization takes a real-life approach to the questions and issues around sex and sexuality that matter most to Canadians. It provides accurate, credible, and up-to-date information and education on topics related to sexual and reproductive health ranging from sex to lifestyle choices, contraception awareness, and sexually transmitted infections.

The STD Project

Website: https://www.thestdproject.com

Facebook and Twitter: @thestdproject

Instagram: @jenellemariepierce

An organization that works to achieve STD prevention by eradicating the stigma surrounding STDs. The group raises awareness and acceptance of STDs through story-telling and resources.

Trip Project

Toronto, Canada

Website: http://www.tripproject.ca

Facebook: @TRIPProject

Twitter: @tripproject

Trip provides several services to the Toronto rave community and beyond. The project is known for its onsite outreach booths and a vendor-style setup staffed by youth outreach workers and volunteers offering a display of safer drug use and safer sex information and supplies such as earplugs, condoms, lube, and needle exchange services.

FOR FURTHER READING

Albright, Kendra S., Karen W. Gavigan, and Sarah J. Petrulis. *AIDS in the End Zone.* Columbia, SC: University of South Carolina Press, 2014.

Ambrose, Marylou. *Sexually Transmitted Diseases: Examining STDs* (Diseases, Disorders, Symptoms). Berkeley Heights, NJ: Enslow Publishers, 2015.

Bailey, Jacqui, and Jan McCafferty. *Sex, Puberty and All That Stuff: A Guide to Growing Up.* Hauppauge, NY: Barron's, 2013.

De Meza, Lesley, and Stephen De Silva. *The A-Z of Growing Up, Puberty and Sex.* London: Franklin Watts, 2014.

Henderson, Elisabeth, and Nancy Armstrong. *100 Questions You'd Never Ask Your Parents: Straight Answers to Teens' Questions About Sex, Sexuality, and Health.* New York: Roaring Brook Press, 2013.

Honders, Christine. *The Dangers of Sexually Transmitted Diseases* (Diseases and Disorders Series). New York: Lucent Press, 2018.

Hunter, Miranda, and William Hunter. *Sexually Transmitted Infections* (Young Adult's Guide to the Science of Health). Philadelphia, PA: Mason Crest Publishers, 2014.

McPartland, Randall. *HIV and AIDS* (Deadliest Diseases of All Time). New York: Cavendish Square, 2016.

Salinas, Claudia Meléndez. *A Fighting Chance.* Houston, TX: Piñata Books, 2015.

Verdi, Jessica. *My Life After Now.* Naperville, IL: Sourcebooks Fire, 2013.

American Sexual Health Association. "Get Tested."
Retrieved March 6, 2018. http://www.ashasexualhealth
.org/stdsstis/get-tested.

Anderson-Minshall, Jacob. "Shocking Stats on STDs in
America." Plus, September 25, 2015. https://www
.hivplusmag.com/prevention/2015/09/25/shocking
-stats-stds-america.

AVERT. "Unprotected Sex and HIV." November 23,
2017. https://www.avert.org/hiv-transmission
-prevention/unprotected-sex.

Centers for Disease Control and Prevention. "CDC Fact
Sheet: Reported STDs in the United States, 2016."
National Center for HIV/AIDS, Viral Hepatitis, STD,
and TB Prevention, September 2017. https://www
.cdc.gov/nchhstp/newsroom/docs/factsheets/std
-trends-508.pdf.

Centers for Disease Control and Prevention. "Condom
Effectiveness." National Center for HIV/AIDS, Viral
Hepatitis, STD, and TB Prevention, September 7,
2017. https://www.cdc.gov/condomeffectiveness
/index.html.

Cosmopolitan. "What Living with an STI Is Really Like."
October 14, 2014. https://www.cosmopolitan.com
/sex-love/news/a32050/living-with-an-sti.

Department of Health. "STD & HIV Facts." State of
New York, March 2013. https://www.health.ny.gov
/publications/9111.pdf.

NHS Choices. "HIV and AIDS." NHS, July 17, 2017. https://www.nhs.uk/conditions/hiv-and-aids/prevention.

Pierce, Jenelle Marie. "The Truth About Whether You Can Get an STI From a Toilet Seat." *Allure*, August 17, 2017. https://www.allure.com/story/can-you-get-an-sti-from-a-toilet-seat.

Planned Parenthood. "All About Sex." Retrieved March 6, 2018. https://www.plannedparenthood.org/learn/teens/sex/all-about-sex.

Planned Parenthood. "Withdrawal (Pull-Out Method)." Retrieved March 6, 2018. https://www.plannedparenthood.org/learn/birth-control/withdrawal-pull-out-method.

RAINN. "Steps You Can Take After Sexual Assault." Retrieved March 6, 2018. https://www.rainn.org/articles/steps-you-can-take-after-sexual-assault.

Terrence Higgins Trust. "Condoms." Retrieved March 6, 2018. http://www.tht.org.uk/sexual-health/Improving-your-sexual-health/Condoms.

Terrence Higgins Trust. "Ways HIV Is Not Transmitted." Retrieved March 6, 2018. http://www.tht.org.uk/sexual-health/About-HIV/How-HIV-is-transmitted/Ways-HIV-is-not-transmitted.

Terrence Higgins Trust. "What Are STIs?" Retrieved March 6, 2018. http://www.tht.org.uk/sexual-health/About-STIs/What-are-STIs_qm_.

Terrence Higgins Trust. "Unprotected Sex and HIV." Retrieved March 6, 2018. http://www.tht.org.uk/sexual-health/Improving-your-sexual-health/Unprotected-sex.

THINX. "The Truth About Living With an STI." Nov 26, 2016. https://www.shethinx.com/blogs/womens -health/the-truth-about-living-with-an-sti.

US Department of Health & Human Services. "HIV Treatment As Prevention." SMAIF, May 15, 2017. https://www.hiv.gov/hiv-basics/hiv-prevention/using -hiv-medication-to-reduce-risk/hiv-treatment-as -prevention.

US Department of Health & Human Services. "What Are HIV and AIDS?" SMAIF, May 17, 2017. https://www .hiv.gov/hiv-basics/overview/about-hiv-and-aids /what-are-hiv-and-aids.

ABOUT THE AUTHOR

Carolyn DeCarlo is a poet and fiction writer from Baltimore, Maryland, who now lives in New Zealand. She has been a mentor for the ASK Program, serving at-risk youth in the juvenile justice system of Washington, DC, and has volunteered for 826DC. She has a BA in English and psychology from Georgetown University and an MFA in creative writing from the University of Maryland, College Park. She has written several chapbooks, including *Green Place* (*Enjoy Journal*, 2015).

PHOTO CREDITS